Children of the World

England

For a free color catalog describing Gareth Stevens' list of high-quality children's books, call 1-800-341-3569 (USA) or 1-800-461-9120 (Canada).

For their help in the preparation of *Children of the World: England*, the editors gratefully thank Joan Clinton, British Tourist Authority, Chicago, Illinois; Linda Ilsley, Milwaukee, Wisconsin; and Mary Ann Smethers, London, England.

Library of Congress Cataloging-in-Publication Data
Katō, Setsuo.
    England / photography by Setsuo Kato; edited by John O'Brien, Susan Taylor-Boyd, Valerie Weber.
        p.   cm. — (Children of the world)
    Originally published: Tokyo: Kaiseisha. 1989.
    "This work was originally published in shortened form consisting of section 1 only"—Pref.
    Includes index.
    Summary: Presents the life of a ten-year-old boy and his family in London, describing his home and school activities and the religions, foods, political system, language, and ethnic composition of his country.
    ISBN 1-55532-211-5
    1. England—Civilization—Juvenile literature. 2. Children—England—Juvenile literature. [1. England—Social life and customs. 2. Family life—England.] I. O'Brien, John. II. Taylor-Boyd, Susan, 1949- III. Weber, Valerie. IV. Title. V. Series.
DA115.K38 1989
942—dc20   89-4462

North American edition first published in 1990 by

Gareth Stevens Children's Books
RiverCenter Building, Suite 201
1555 North RiverCenter Drive
Milwaukee, Wisconsin 53212, USA

Series editor: Rhoda Irene Sherwood
Research editor: Scott Enk
Map design: Sheri Gibbs

Printed in the United States of America

1 2 3 4 5 6 7 8 9 96 95 94 93 92 91 90

Children of the World

England

Photography
by Setsuo Kato

Edited by
Susan Taylor-Boyd,
John O'Brien, &
Valerie Weber

Gareth Stevens Children's Books
MILWAUKEE

. . . a note about *Children of the World*:

The children of the world live in fishing towns, Arctic regions, and urban centers, on islands and in mountain valleys, on sheep ranches and fruit farms. This series follows one child in each country through the pattern of his or her life. Candid photographs show the children with their families, at school, at play, and in their communities. The text describes the dreams of the children and, often through their own words, tells how they see themselves and their lives.

Each book also explores events that are unique to the country in which the child lives, including festivals, religious ceremonies, and holidays. The *Children of the World* series does more than tell about foreign countries. It introduces the children of each country and shows readers what it is like to be a child in that country.

. . . and about *England*:

England, part of the island of Great Britain, is also a major part of the nation now called the United Kingdom. Ben lives in the capital of the United Kingdom, London. His favorite activities are soccer and cricket, two popular English sports.

To enhance this book's value in libraries and classrooms, comprehensive reference sections include up-to-date information about England's geography, demographics, language, currency, education, culture, industry, and natural resources. *England* also features a bibliography, research topics, activity projects, and discussions of such subjects as London, the country's history, political system, ethnic and religious composition, and language.

The living conditions and experiences of children in England vary tremendously according to economic, environmental, and ethnic circumstances. The reference sections help bring to life for young readers the diversity and richness of the culture and heritage of England. Of particular interest are discussions of England's influence in the development of the New World, its constitutional monarchy, and Parliament.

CONTENTS

Ben's family is ready to go on a trip to the country. From left: Tom; Ben's mother, Mary Ann, holding Nick; his father, Mike; and Ben.

LIVING IN ENGLAND:
Ben, an Enthusiastic Athlete

Ben, short for Benjamin, is ten. He lives with his family in London, the capital of England. His neighborhood, Muswell Hill, is in the northern part of the city. Ben's parents, Mike and Mary Ann Smethers, are both 39. Ben also has two brothers, Tom, age 13, and Nick, age 1.

Ben's quiet street. His house was built one hundred years ago. Most English houses are built of bricks so they will last three or four hundred years.

Ben's Family and Neighborhood

Ben's house looks like many other houses in London. These terrace houses all share side walls and windows face only the street and a small backyard. While all the homes in each row seem alike, each family makes its home special by painting its front door a different color or by choosing different shrubs for the front yard. The backyard of Ben's home is big enough for a garden for Mum, the children's name for Mary Ann — she keeps flowers blooming in all seasons.

Ben's house has two stories. The living room, kitchen, and family room are on the ground floor. Upstairs are three bedrooms and a bathroom. Ben and Tom each have their own room. Ben's room is larger than Tom's because when Nick is older, he will share Ben's room. In the meantime, the boys use Ben's room as their playroom.

Ben's house in London. In the background, you can see modern apartment houses.

Typical English urban houses. Land is scarce in the cities, so the houses are built close together.

Ben lives in a quiet neighborhood filled with trees, flowers, and lawns. He loves to roller-skate around his block or to ride his bicycle to the parks scattered around London. This enormous city with an area population of over ten million is renowned for its many green spaces such as parks, squares, and heath, which is open, uncultivated ground.

A short walk away from Ben's home is the old Alexandra Palace, where the British Broadcasting Corporation has its television studios. Nearby is the wooded area of Highgate, a great place for playing or walking. Sometimes Ben goes to Waterlow Park to feed the rabbits, goats, and deer.

Dad's job is to carve the turkey.

Celebrating Christmas

Christmas is one of the happiest times of the year for English children. Ben gets many gifts and he loves the special treats. So the closer Christmas comes, the more excited Ben gets. Some of his friends still think that Father Christmas (the English name for Santa Claus) comes down the chimneys and brings them presents, but Ben doesn't believe that anymore.

"New roller skates! Just what I wanted."

Ben clears the table quickly since dessert awaits.

The traditional Christmas dessert — plum pudding.

The Church of England, a Protestant branch of Christianity, is the official religion in England. Ben sometimes goes to church, but Ben's parents aren't very religious. They celebrate Christmas because it's a chance for all the family to get together. Mum comes from a family of five children, so there are many relatives — and many presents to open! This year Ben got new roller skates. He broke his old pair trying to jump over a box on the sidewalk, so he is happy to have new ones.

Christmas dinner is something special to anticipate. There is always a turkey, and Mum spends days making delicious food and treats. But best of all is the Christmas pudding for dessert. The aromas from baking and cooking fill the house. By the end of the meal, everyone is drowsy from all the food. But Ben and Tom still help to clear the table and to wash the dishes.

11

Off to the park!

Grandma takes time for a visit.

Mum also gets a chance to try out the skates.

Ben enjoys a quiet time feeding Nick.

Having Fun at Home

Ben is the middle brother. He and Tom are only three years apart in age, so they often play together. But Ben and Nick are nine years apart, and Nick still can't walk or talk. When Mum is busy or guests come, Ben helps look after the baby. Ben gives Nick his milk and plays with him. When Ben pulls the pram, or baby carriage, from the hallway, Nick grins and gurgles, ready for their walk.

Ben builds a truck with his Lego pieces.

Ben's collection of cat knickknacks.

Ben occasionally plays with friends in the neighborhood, but in winter, the night comes so early that it is often dark by the time the children get home from school. So indoor games are popular after school. In summer, when the days are longer, most children go to sports clubs where they play games like cricket and tennis.

The two brothers ponder their next moves.

Computer games are Ben's favorite.

A friendly snooker game.

Ben takes piano lessons.

Ben retrieves Rascal.

After school, Ben and Tom sometimes enjoy watching videos. But more often, they play games like Monopoly, backgammon, computer games, and snooker, a game like pool. Tom usually wins but Ben sometimes wins at backgammon. If Ben loses too often, he'll cheat by moving Tom's pieces. When Tom catches him, he shouts, "That's not fair!" But the boys rarely get into fights.

Once a week, Ben has a piano lesson from a teacher who lives in his neighborhood. He's been taking lessons for a year, but he's still struggling. The teacher tells him that he has talent but should practice more, at least 45 minutes every day. He would rather be playing computer games.

Ben also loves animals. He has a cage of gerbils in his room and their squeaking sometimes keeps him awake at night. He's also in charge of caring for the family cat, a black tomcat named Rascal. Ben is careful not to let Rascal around when the gerbils are out racing on the floor of his bedroom.

These gerbils require lots of attention.

When the snow comes, it's time to build a snowman.

An Unexpected Snowfall

Snow is a wonderful treat. But there is seldom much of it, and what there is stays on the ground for only a few days, except in the hilly and mountainous areas in the north of England. In London, snow comes so rarely that Nick and Tom always want to rush outside to enjoy the snow before it melts.

The boys bundle up with some extra layers of clothes, and Mum always reminds them to put on their hats, gloves, and boots, which they call wellies, short for Wellington boots. Tom and Ben go to a nearby park to build a snowman and to sled. Soon, children from the neighborhood join them, shouting and throwing snowballs.

Although the snow is not deep, there is enough for a good sled race.

The weather in London is mild. Summer high temperatures average about 73°F (23°C). Minimum temperatures in the center of London are two to three degrees higher than in the surrounding countryside because of the warmth from heated buildings.

London gets an average of 23 inches (58 cm) of rainfall a year, about the same amount as Portland, Oregon. But the city has many gray days, when skies are overcast with rain clouds. London only averages about seven hours of sunlight a day in spring and early summer.

London used to be known as a city of almost perpetual fog. Old Sherlock Holmes movies, for example, showed him seeking clues in dank and foggy streets. Much of the fog was caused by people burning soft coal to heat their homes. This coal produced sulfur fumes that combined with moisture in the air to form smog. Laws forbidding the use of this coal to heat homes resulted in much clearer air.

The boys return home with their sleds.

In winter, the daylight hours are often clear and crisp. That's because the winds blow away the smog and clouds that often hang over the city. Some winter days may be below 32°F (0°C), but the average winter temperatures are between 35°F and 44°F (2°C-7°C).

Sometimes the whole family goes for a walk in the snow after supper. Mum bundles up Nick in his padded snowsuit, which makes him so round he can hardly move. Ben and Tom take turns pulling a sled down the dimly lit street with Nick propped upright in it. Ben and Tom love to see the city all white and glistening beneath the lights at night.

Occasionally, they end their walk with a visit to the local fish and chips shop for an evening snack. Fish and chips, the English word for French fries, has long been the traditional English meal. Like many English people, Ben likes to eat his fish with malt vinegar. His favorite kind of fish is cod.

19

Midday meal at cousin Holly's. The English often eat their big meal in the middle of the day.

Special Activities

Holly, a cousin, is a year younger than Tom and also lives in London. Her mother, Lucy, is Mary Ann's twin sister. The sisters are very close and meet at one or the other's house at least once a month.

The English love dessert, which they call a sweet or pudding.

The boys and Holly watch a Madonna music video.

Preparing for the weekly newspaper route.

Delivering papers at terrace houses.

Ben's hands are black from the newspaper ink.

When the family visits Holly's house, the boys often watch music videos. Holly's favorite is Madonna, but Ben would rather listen to other pop music. He also enjoys watching music shows on television and tries not to miss a night of a program called "EastEnders." This drama follows the lives of working-class people in the East End of London, probing topics such as drug abuse, teen pregnancy, and problems of the young and old. In recent years, it has been the highest-rated program in all of England.

Many people buy their newspapers from newsstands, and on Thursday nights, Ben and Tom deliver one of the weekly local papers. Supplied free to every house, it is packed with advertisements. The boys' newspaper route includes almost 100 houses in the neighborhood. It takes Ben and Tom about two hours to complete their work. Ben earns six pounds (about $10.70) weekly from this job. He rents videos with the money or buys photographs of his favorite British soccer stars.

Ben stays cozy while finishing some schoolwork.

Brush those teeth bright at least twice a day!

Ben's School Day

Ben's school day starts at seven o'clock in the morning. Sometimes he wakes up by himself, but usually he needs the sharp ringing of the alarm clock. On cold, dark winter mornings, it is especially difficult to leave his warm bed, but he sluggishly pulls himself out when Mum calls him.

It's a ten-minute walk to school.

He washes his face and wolfs down breakfast — cold cereal or toast, fruit juice, and tea, an extremely popular beverage in England. The English consume an average of about eight and a half pounds (4 kg) of tea per year per person! Once Ben has finished his tea, he feels that the day has begun. He used to have bacon and eggs too, but recently Mum has stopped making them. Ben likes bacon but he hates eggs.

Ben checks his school bag each morning.

Ben's school, Muswell Hill Junior School.

Ben is good at rounders, a game like baseball.

Ben's school is the Muswell Hill Junior School, which is within walking distance of his house. Most of the students live near the school and walk, but a few children are driven there by their parents. Ben's school is for children from the ages of seven to eleven. There are 188 students in eight classes, two classes for each form, or grade. Ben is in the third year, and there are 24 students in his class. His teacher is Pat Lowe.

Students work in groups for lessons. Here they are working on art projects.

Mrs. Lowe, Ben's teacher, works with him on a lesson.

Some examples of their artwork.

Ben's drawing of a squirrel.

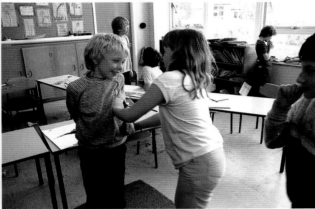

Playing with a friend during a break.

Ben's favorite class — drawing.

At Ben's junior school, lessons are informal. Desks are not lined up in rows but are pushed together in small groups. Even these groupings aren't usually rigid; the students can rearrange them as they wish.

The teacher rarely uses the blackboard. Instead she moves around among the children giving each child personal attention. This is called an integrated day program, a program in which children learn at their own pace rather than follow a prescribed schedule of classes. This method of teaching is becoming popular throughout England.

Sometimes the children start talking to each other as soon as the teacher moves away, but this is not allowed. Mrs. Lowe corrects them with a stern voice. Sometimes she has to tell Ben to stop chatting about soccer. Ben doesn't like English and arithmetic, but he enjoys drawing, crafts, and physical education.

Waiting to enter school.

The children's favorite part of the school day is the lunch break. The noisy dining room is filled with students from all the grades. Time flies as the children eat their lunch and talk about television and plans for summer.

More than half of the children buy school lunches for 50 pence (about 90¢). Children whose parents are unemployed receive their lunches for free. The other children bring lunches from home.

At Ben's school, children are not allowed to take candy in their packed lunches. They usually bring sandwiches, fruit, yogurt, and potato chips.

Ben has a friend from India named Paresh. Sometimes he likes to try Paresh's lunch. Often Paresh brings *chapatis*, a type of bread, instead of a sandwich. Ben's favorite chapatis are filled with curried chicken with spices such as coriander, pepper, and cardamon. It's quite spicy compared to most English food, which doesn't require many spices. Ben grabs his fruit juice when the food gets too hot for his taste buds, and Paresh laughs at his expression.

There is malt vinegar on the table, in case anyone brought fish and chips.

After lunch, Ben and his friends run out to the playground and practice soccer. Too soon they are called back in for more lessons. Today Ben's class is studying the human body and how it fights disease. While Ben enjoys tracing the diagram of the circulation system in his workbook, he is looking forward to the end of the school day. His eyes keep wandering to the clock.

On most days, school finishes around 3:30 p.m. unless the class takes a field trip, when they may be delayed. Ben loves going to the British Museum and gazing at the antiquities from faraway lands. He dreams of traveling and exploring the countries and ancient ruins these treasures were taken from. But travel will have to wait.

In England, education is compulsory from age 5 to age 16. Elementary state-run education is composed of infant's school (ages 5 to 7) and junior school (from ages 7 to 11), while secondary education consists of comprehensive school (from ages 11 to 18). Tom is in the second year of comprehensive school.

Many students leave the comprehensive school at age 16 and look for work. But some students stay in school for two more years and study for their university entrance examination. Government grants are available to all university students, as they are not allowed to work their way through college.

Playing soccer during the lunch break.

Besides the state-run system of education, England also has a private system that is quite different. This private system has schools called "public schools." Parents must pay tuition for their children to attend these schools.

Some "public schools" have only students who board at the school or students who are there only during the day. Others have a combination of boarding and day students. "Public schools" take children from the ages of 11 to 13 up to ages 18 or 19.

The traditions and high standards of education of some of these schools are well known, even outside England. In the past, only English boys from the nobility and wealthy upper class attended "public schools." Now the schools accept students from around the world, especially from England's former colonies.

Most of the students from these private schools go on to a university. Private elementary schools, called prep schools, prepare children for entrance to these "public schools."

Ben's classmates and Mrs. Lowe (in the back).

The state-run schools are open Monday through Friday, leaving the weekends free. Each state-run school year consists of three terms. The first term runs from September until Christmas. The second term runs from January until Easter. The third term runs from Easter until the middle of July. There are vacations at the end of each term and a week-long vacation in the middle of each term. The summer vacation is the longest and lasts six weeks.

Packing for a trip.

Summer Travel

At last, summer vacation! For many years, Ben's family has gone to a beach in Devon, in southwestern England. About 185 miles (300 km) from London, Devon is a famous resort area with a beautiful coastline, pastoral scenery, and the wide uplands of Dartmoor. Ben has traveled throughout England, but he is fond of Devon with its rolling green countryside and beaches.

An English highway, called a motorway. The English drive on the left side of the road.

Dartmoor in Devon. You can still see wild ponies there.

With three boys sitting in the back, the van is a bit cramped. The trunk, called a "boot" in England, is packed with everything from Nick's pram to skateboards, Frisbees, tennis rackets, cricket bats, games, buckets, and shovels. Once they have passed Heathrow Airport and Windsor Castle, they begin to see rural scenery. A warm August breeze blows through the open windows, bringing the smell of summer.

Sheep are plentiful in Devon.

31

"Look out! Here comes another one."

Playing games on the beach.

Although there are amusement parks at some beaches, at most English beach resorts there is only the beach itself. Many beaches in Devon are of sand, but other resort areas have beaches of stone. People spend their summer there sunbathing, reading, swimming, and playing the entire day. Many English people go to the beach during summer vacation, not only to English resorts, but also to resorts in Spain, Greece, and France.

As soon as they arrive at the beach, Mum and Dad sit down to read and play with Nick. Ben and Tom, though, can't sit still. They splash in the sea, look for shells, play cricket on the beach, and build sand castles all day long.

Inhabited since the Bronze Age, Devon retains numerous reminders of 5,000 years of history. Sometimes the family piles into the car and visits Exmoor and Dartmoor national parks, with their prehistoric relics such as hill forts, hut circles, standing stones, and barrows, which are large mounds of stones or earth piled on ancient burial sites.

Devon was also supposedly the home of the legendary King Arthur. Camelford, in north-western Devon, claims to have been the site of Camelot, the capital of his kingdom. Tom and Ben sometimes pretend to be Knights of the Round Table, off on some thrilling quest.

These activities help them relax and forget about school. When the holidays are over, Ben will go into the fourth year, the highest grade in junior school.

There's even a donkey to ride!

"I wonder how far I can throw my Frisbee."

The crowning touches to a sand castle.

"Look at me. I'm Tarzan."

An afternoon tea of scones and Devonshire cream, a time to dream about the future.

Ben's Dreams

Next year Ben's family is going to spend the summer in the United States, where another of Mum's sisters lives. Ben enjoys travel. He has been to France and Belgium and has his own passport. One of Ben's dreams is to travel to many countries when he grows up. Because he likes to draw, he would like to make sketches of the places he visits.

Another of Ben's dreams is to go on to a university. Only those students at state schools who like to study and get good grades can consider further education. Dad and Mum make sure that Tom and Ben do their homework. They hope that both boys will go on to study at a university, but they say it is up to Ben and Tom themselves to choose their careers. This attitude is fairly common among English parents.

Skateboarding develops balance, a necessity for a future soccer champion.

Ben concentrates on his draughts (checkers) game.

Ben's greatest dream is to be a professional soccer player when he grows up. He longs to play in the final of the Football Association Cup and go up to the Royal Box to receive the trophy for his team. Tom's dream is to be a cricketer. Many English boys share similar hopes of athletic glory. Most of them aspire to play either soccer or cricket, the most popular English sports.

Oxford Street in London. Taxis, double-decker buses, and bikes share the road with automobiles.

London

The center of London is only about 30 minutes away on the underground (subway) from Ben's neighborhood. Ben and Tom go downtown about eight times a year. Ben's favorite times have been when Dad took the boys to a movie or a musical or when Ben has gone to the British Museum or the National Gallery on a school field trip.

In London's center, Piccadilly Circus is the gathering place for visitors from all over the world. Every day crowds congregate to watch the changing of the guard at Buckingham Palace, the queen of England's residence in London. Department stores and specialty shops line Oxford Street and Regent Street, world-famous retail areas. Police officers called "bobbies" slowly walk around on their patrol.

The boys also like to travel by double-decker bus.

A hamburger at Wimpy's, the English equivalent of McDonald's.

Ben and Tom sit at Piccadilly Circus. In England, *circus* means a circular area.

The London underground, or "tube," can take you almost anywhere in the city.

Not long ago, Ben went with his dad to see the musical *Time*, a science fiction production with marvelous stage effects and music. Besides the theater, Ben especially likes going to Hamleys of Regent Street, Ltd., a huge toy shop that has anything from lead soldiers to computer games. Ben can spend a whole day there without getting bored.

Family Fun

Today Ben and his family are meeting Holly and her family so they can all go to the pool in Fulham, a nearby suburb. Ben likes this large indoor swimming center, with its 50-meter (164 ft) competition pool, the diving pool, and the pool with slides and lots of play equipment.

Holly adores swimming, and is totally at ease in the water. Even though Ben is athletic, he is not comfortable swimming and won't let go of his float. Tom and Holly have great fun on the diving boards, jumping into the pool over and over again.

A stream of water rushes down the curving water slide. The children can pick up quite a bit of speed coming down. Mum has tried the slide, and at the end, she lies down and goes into the pool headfirst. The children laugh at the sight of her shooting down into the water, and Mum splashes them when she comes up for air.

Sitting in the balcony overlooking the pool, Dad would rather watch Nick and read his newspaper. When Nick gets older, Ben is looking forward to going down the slide with him.

Swimming at the Fulham pool is a family outing.

On an "island" in Fulham pool. Mum is on the right, Aunt Lucy is on the left, and Holly is next to Tom.

Nick is happy just playing with his feet.

The alligator guards its own waterfall.

Dad takes the boys to soccer matches almost every month.

Ben shows off his soccer card collection.

Ben, the Sports Spectator and Participant

Both Ben and Tom are thrilled when Dad agrees to take them to the "local derby," a soccer match between local teams. Today, two of London's top teams, both among the best in the country, are competing for the regional championship. Ben's favorite team, Chelsea, is playing against Tom's favorite team, Arsenal. Ben knows all the players, but he likes the Chelsea forward, Kerry Dixon, best and eagerly collects pictures of him. Ben wears a blue scarf, the Chelsea color, and Tom wears a red one, the Arsenal color.

As the boys walk to the stadium, they argue heatedly about which team is better, keeping watch for a glimpse of their favorite soccer star. At a game last month, Ben got an autograph from the Chelsea goalie and he is still talking about it. Tom claims the autograph isn't worth anything because the goalie is mediocre.

Ben and Tom try to see their favorite players warming up.

The stadium is packed with boisterous fans who occasionally bellow out the team song to encourage their side on to victory. The two teams are evenly matched and each goalie determinedly defends his net. The ball is constantly in motion, so each player must quickly adjust his strategy accordingly.

At the intermission, Tom and Ben meet with other friends to swap soccer cards, photographs of soccer players from around the country. They discuss how their favorite teams are doing in the league competition and whether an English team will make it to the World Cup Finals to play against teams from all over the world.

Ben cheers on his Chelsea team loudly, but they lose to Arsenal, so of course, Tom is excited. Ben fights back tears of disappointment.

A soccer team consists of 11 players. The object in soccer is to score goals by getting the soccer ball into the opposing team's goal, a large net at each end of the field. The field in soccer is about a third larger than a North American football field. A soccer match has two 45-minute playing periods. At the end of the match, the team with the most goals wins. If each team has the same number of points, the game is declared a draw.

Each team has a goalie who protects the goal. Only goalies can use their hands or arms to move the ball, and then only within the goal area. All other team members are forbidden to use their hands or arms; they must use only their feet, chest, or head to hit the ball or the referee will call a penalty. Soccer players develop skillful methods for moving the ball down the soccer field. Some players can pick the ball up with their feet and "throw" it to another teammate by kicking their feet out behind them.

The stadium is sold-out for the match between Arsenal and Chelsea.

Soccer is said to be the world's most popular sport. Although it was invented in England, soccer has developed an avid following all over Europe and South America. It has also become more popular in the United States and Canada.

Part of its popularity probably stems from the fact that it requires little equipment, only a ball. Goals can be marked with chalk on any rough surface. Soccer can even be played barefoot!

In England, many cities sponsor one or more professional teams that compete for a national championship. Fans are extremely loyal to their chosen team, which isn't always the team from their city. Ben chose his team because he likes the players. Other people choose a team because of its success.

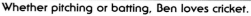
Whether pitching or batting, Ben loves cricket.

Ben is an enthusiastic athlete. He plays many different sports, but he is best at cricket, a traditional English sport played with a flat bat and a hard ball. It is a little like baseball, but there are two pitching and batting positions in cricket instead of one. Both professional and amateur teams compete in cricket. Ben is a member of the North Middlesex Under Eleven team, the children's cricket team based at Muswell Hill. The cricket season lasts from April to October, and every Sunday there are matches lasting two to three hours.

When the cricket season is over, the soccer season starts. All the children in Ben's cricket club play soccer in winter. Ben has no specific position in soccer yet, but he would like to be an offensive player.

The English often play tennis on grass courts.

Ben and Tom enjoy spending a day playing golf with Dad.

Every Sunday Ben has tennis lessons. He has just started, but his coach says Ben could be good because of his experience in playing cricket.

Sometimes Dad takes Tom and Ben to the golf course in a park near their house where they practice. Somehow, Ben has developed an awkward golfing style because he holds the club wrong. No matter how many times Dad tells him, Ben can't change his hand position. "It's the easiest way to hit," he says, showing an unexpected stubborn streak. But this confusion did lead to an interesting discovery. Ben writes, throws a ball, and holds his tennis racket with his right hand, but in cricket he is a left-handed batter. So it's no wonder he's confused when golfing!

Ben's Birthday

Ben's birthday is on October 28 and Tom's is on October 27, so for Mum's convenience, they always have their party on the same day. This year they hold the party on Ben's birthday, and the boys invite friends they have in common from the soccer team. Crowding into the house, their teammates wish Ben and Tom a happy birthday.

Everyone wants to watch the soccer match.

On the table are sandwiches, cupcakes, sausages, and other kinds of food the boys like. Two birthday cakes stand side by side, one with ten candles for Ben and one with thirteen for Tom. First Ben gets to blow out the candles on his chocolate cake. Then Tom takes a big breath and blows his candles out.

Even Ben's birthday cake has soccer players on it.

Ben is growing up happy and relaxed. Most English families do not seem to be strict about discipline. Many parents do not pressure their children and respect their decisions. Teachers at school follow a similar path. They look for what is individual in each child and encourage the child in that direction.

Now this is the way to celebrate a birthday!

The Houses of Parliament, seen from the Thames River.

FOR YOUR INFORMATION: England

Official Name: England

Capital: London

History

Prehistoric England and Invasions

Primitive peoples lived in England during the Stone Age over 500,000 years ago. A series of European peoples then began to colonize the island. The Beaker people arrived from central Europe around 3500 BC. Centuries later, between 800 and 500 BC, the Celts came from Germany and France in large numbers. In 55 BC, the Romans, led by Julius Caesar, first came to England. Roman influence spread across the island, and for over four centuries, the Romans brought peace and prosperity and, by the early 4th century, Christianity. But in about 400 AD, they left to defend their declining empire in mainland Europe.

Their departure left England open to attacks from other European peoples such as the Angles and Saxons, who settled and intermarried with the English and largely suppressed Christianity. In the 7th century, missionaries came to convert people to Catholicism. During the 9th and 10th centuries, Norwegian, Swedish, and Danish marauders, known as Vikings, also invaded.

In 1066, Normans from France made the last successful foreign invasion of England. William, Duke of Normandy, defeated the Anglo-Saxon king, Harold II, at the Battle of Hastings. William the Conqueror, as he is called, unified England and promoted agriculture, industry, commerce, law, and government.

The Magna Carta and Parliament

But not all subsequent monarchs were effective or just. King John, for example, tried to reduce the power of barons and church leaders. In 1215, they forced him to sign the Magna Carta, "Great Charter," in which he promised to respect current laws and basic human rights. Later, democracy took stronger root as kings began to share their powers with other leaders, such as nobles and wealthy merchants, who represented some segments of the population. They made decisions in a group that was to become the earliest form of England's Parliament.

Struggles for Control of Church and Throne

Henry VIII, who ruled from 1509 to 1547, also struggled to reduce the power of the church. Henry VIII wanted to divorce his first wife because she had borne no son to succeed him. Since the pope refused to annul his first marriage, the king abolished the Catholic church in England and established the Church of England with himself as leader. He divorced his first wife and married Anne Boleyn, whom he later executed. Over the next ten years, he had four more wives.

The struggle over the national religion and control of the government continued for over a century. When Henry VIII's daughter Mary I became monarch, she restored Catholicism and persecuted the Protestants, supporters of the Church of England who had resisted the return to Catholicism. At her death, her half-sister Elizabeth I reinstated the Church of England. To ensure its dominance, Elizabeth had her Catholic cousin Mary, who was next in line for the throne, executed.

The king of Spain, Philip II, also wanted to restore England to Catholicism and to replace Elizabeth as ruler. In 1588, he sent a huge fleet of ships, the Armada, to invade England. But under the leadership of Sir Francis Drake, the English navy destroyed the Armada. This victory created a strong sense of national pride. During the Elizabethan Age (1558-1603), England gained respect worldwide and achieved artistic and literary greatness at home.

Charles I became king in 1625 and began to pursue unpopular governmental and religious policies. He tried to rule without the support of Parliament, now composed mainly of wealthy landowners and merchants. By 1642, he had raised new taxes without Parliament's consent and dissolved several Parliaments because they didn't comply with his desires. He also discriminated against the Puritans, a religious minority who wanted to eliminate any vestige of Catholic influence from the Church of England. These actions caused increasing dissent in Parliament and the country.

Finally, despite the protests of most English people, both Charles and Parliament drafted soldiers. Charles, the nobility, and the Royalist forces, called Cavaliers, were led by the king's nephew, Prince Rupert. Oliver Cromwell, a Puritan, headed Parliament's army, called Roundheads because of their haircuts. Parliament's army defeated the Royalists and captured the king. In 1649, Charles I was beheaded for treason, and Cromwell became Lord Protector. With the elected members of Parliament, Cromwell created a republic. But after Cromwell's death in 1658, the government crumbled, and Parliament placed Charles II on his father's throne.

England Extends Its Empire

With England's Civil War over, the country began to extend trade and gain colonies overseas. England's influence in North America began in the early 17th century. English settlers found the West Indies and the southern areas of North America ideal for growing tobacco, rice, and sugar cane, but they needed an inexpensive work force to raise these crops. By the end of the century, a cycle of trade in slaves and agricultural products grew.

During this time, American colonists grew increasingly angry because they were paying heavy taxes but were not allowed to vote in Parliament. These taxes supported English wars to wrest control of Canada and India from the French. So the colonists rebelled and, by 1781, they won the last decisive battle.

The loss of the American colonies changed the focus of English goals for growth. England now tried to gain new territory in Asia and Africa and to expand its existing colonies in North America and India. In the 18th and 19th centuries, this far-reaching empire gained new territories in the Mediterranean, the Caribbean, Canada, Australia, Asia, and Africa.

The Industrial Revolution

At the same time as the American Revolution, an industrial revolution transformed England's economy from an agricultural one into the world's first industrial economy. This revolution was based on the country's rich mineral resources, especially coal and iron ore, and on easy access to raw materials from its colonies.

This period saw a series of mechanical inventions that dramatically changed the way people lived and worked, starting with the spinning and weaving industries. It also saw enormous progress in science and in industries such as mining, transportation, and shipbuilding. Machines replaced human skills. But industrial progress did not mean human progress. The new owners of industry became rich while other adults and children slaved long hours for low wages and often lived in slums.

The Napoleonic Wars and the Victorian Era

Although the United Kingdom was the most powerful nation on Earth at this time, it had had one chief rival and enemy for centuries — France. England saw France's expansion as a threat to both its independence and its own growing empire. Napoleon Bonaparte, who crowned himself emperor of France in 1804, waged war on Europe. His armies defeated Germany, Italy, and Austria and later invaded Spain and Russia. This expansion isolated England from its European markets, so England rebelled. In 1815, the British, under the Duke of Wellington and with the aid of the Prussians, defeated the French army at the Battle of Waterloo.

From then on, England's power grew. During her long reign from 1837 to 1901, Queen Victoria ruled over an empire larger and wealthier than any in previous history. Inventions like railroads, steam power, and industrial machinery helped make England part of the world's leading industrial nation. The British Navy guarded a worldwide empire, while the English language and English literature extended the empire's influence even further.

World War I: 1914-18

During the late 19th and early 20th centuries, Germany grew more powerful and began to build a navy to rival England's own. England saw this as a threat to its shipping industry. So England joined with France and Russia in the Triple Entente. When World War I broke out in 1914, the Triple Entente countries, along with Canada and Japan, fought against the Central Powers, consisting of Germany, Turkey, Bulgaria, and the Austro-Hungarian Empire. Over the next three years, countries such as Italy and Romania joined the Triple Entente countries, now called the Allies. In 1917, in response to the torpedoing of several ships, the US joined the Allies. In 1918, the Allies defeated the Central Powers.

England paid a high price for helping to defeat the Central Powers. More than one in ten Englishmen under the age of 45 died in the war. England's national debt increased while, after a brief boom, unemployment soared. Although the British Empire gained some colonies previously ruled by Germany, other British colonies became self-governing. Economic and political unrest in Europe led to the creation of another empire, a German one — and, by 1939, another world war.

World War II: 1939-45

During the 1930s, Adolf Hitler rose to power in Germany. He sought to conquer much of Europe, so his armies invaded Austria, Czechoslovakia, and finally Poland. To defend Poland, Britain and France declared war against Germany. By 1940, Italy and Japan had joined Germany and formed the Axis countries. Soon, the Germans occupied France.

With France under German rule, Britain stood virtually alone for a time in trying to stop Hitler. Winston Churchill became prime minister in 1940, and his stirring speeches rallied the nation. Later that year, German planes frequently bombed England's major cities in the "blitz," as it was called. During bombing raids, while people in London took refuge in subways and air raid shelters, pilots of the tiny Royal Air Force fought back vastly superior numbers of German planes. This ten-month conflict, known as the Battle of Britain, forced Hitler to abandon his plans to invade England.

But Hitler and his armies continued to wage war on Europe. The USSR and other countries joined England in its fight against the Axis powers. The English also fought in the Far East against Japan. Many English prisoners died while held in Japanese prisoner-of-war camps or while building railroads for the Japanese through the jungles of Asia.

In 1944, the Allies, including Canada, England, and the US, invaded France, and the final drive to liberate Europe began. The following year, the Allies defeated the Axis countries.

Empire in Decline

The two world wars were costly for Britain. Its colonies continued to break away from the empire and later formed the Commonwealth of Nations, an association of independent nations. The Commonwealth includes countries like India, Australia, Canada, and New Zealand. Almost all of Britain's former colonies in Africa, Asia, and the Caribbean are also now independent.

But England is still involved in the affairs of another country — Ireland. The Republic of Ireland is an independent nation that is largely Catholic. Northern Ireland, or Ulster, remains a part of the United Kingdom and is largely Protestant. Most of the Protestants in Northern Ireland want to retain its link with England while the Catholic minority wants to join the Republic of Ireland. Although the conflict has been seen as a religious war, the problems are compounded by the fact that the Catholics have felt that the wealthier Protestants have discriminated against them in the areas of housing, employment, and political representation. Terrorists on both sides have injured and killed many people, and, despite many protests, the British army remains as a peacekeeping force.

Government

The Royal Family

England is a constitutional monarchy with a parliamentary government. By law, the monarch is head of state and of the Church of England and commander in chief of the armed forces. In reality, the monarch is merely a symbol of power and national unity. Since 1952, Queen Elizabeth II has been monarch. She and her husband, Prince Philip, also known as the Duke of Edinburgh,

The guards at Buckingham Palace.

have four children. Their eldest, Prince Charles, is the next in line to the throne. Hordes of journalists record the Royal Family's every move, providing pleasure to rabid royalty watchers around the country and the world.

Parliament

Parliament consists of two chambers — a House of Lords and a House of Commons, the supreme governing body. House of Commons members are elected by voters aged 18 or over. General elections must take place at least every five years. The political party with the most seats forms the government and its leader becomes the prime minister, who then appoints a committee known as the Cabinet to help run the country. Most candidates belong either to the Conservative or Labour parties. Traditionally, the Conservatives (or "Tories") represent the interests of the middle and upper classes, while the Labour party supports the interests of the working class.

The House of Lords is more of a forum for debate. While its members cannot make laws, they do review current and proposed legislation. They are also the highest appeals court in the land; people can ask this court to have judgments from lower courts changed. Its almost 1,200 members are called peers. About two-thirds of these peers inherit their position. The monarchy appoints the remainder, in honor of their achievements or so that they will serve as judges.

Besides Parliament, England also has local levels of elected government. These include regional, county, district, and parish (a division of the county) councils. Each can levy taxes to pay for certain services.

Currency

The unit of currency in England is the pound sterling (£). There are 100 pence in a pound. Coins come in denominations of 1, 2, 5, 10, 20, and 50 pence, and one pound. Paper currency is in units of 5, 10, 20, and 50 pounds. They are in different colors and sizes and carry etchings of the queen and famous historical figures.

Education

Children aged 5 through 16 must go to schools sponsored by the local government or to private schools, called "public schools" in England. For those who leave school at 16, the government guarantees a place in a youth training program. But many children stay at school — mostly in state-run schools for pupils of all abilities — and then study for a degree at a university or a technical school.

Students who hope to go to a university start at 14 to prepare up to 11 subjects for an exam, including languages, mathematics, sciences, and history. They will take the test at about age 16. During the last year of this course, they study little else. This system requires a student to decide early in life what interests to pursue.

Language

The first inhabitants of England spoke languages from the Indo-European family of languages. The Angles and Saxons spoke Low German, the Celts spoke Celtic, and the Vikings spoke Old Norse. These "cousin languages" blended well and prevailed in England until the Norman invasion in 1066. The Norman rulers made French the official language, to be used in government, commerce, and literature. By the 14th century, however, French fell into disuse as the English promoted their native tongue. With England's conquest of other lands, English spread throughout the world.

Today, virtually everyone in England speaks English. Those who don't generally live in minority ethnic groups in England's cities, especially London. Many regions also have their own dialects. An English person's pronunciation is often used to identify upbringing and social class.

Religion

The different settlers in England brought their own religions. The Celts, for example, mainly practiced druidism. The Romans first worshipped many gods and later introduced Christianity. The invasions of Angles and Saxons, who worshipped many gods, largely drove out Christianity. But Christianity returned after missionaries like St. Augustine of Canterbury converted the Anglo-Saxons. By the late 7th century, the Catholic church had formed under the control of the pope in Rome. For the next 900 years, many English monarchs had an uneasy relationship with the church as they both competed for power. Finally, influenced by the Reformation, a European religious movement, Henry VIII broke with Rome and established the Church of England. The monarch, not the pope, became the head of the official church.

Today, all religions are officially tolerated. Most churchgoers belong to the Church of England and other Protestant groups such as the Baptists and Methodists. Almost 10% of the population is Roman Catholic. In recent years, groups of immigrants have introduced a wide variety of faiths, including Hinduism and Islam.

Sports and Recreation

England is a land of sports lovers. Soccer, played from August to May, is the national passion. But spectator violence at games now keeps many peaceful fans away. Both at home and abroad, police often arrest rowdy fans for causing trouble.

Rugby is another favorite winter sport, also played in parts of North America. A far less physical game is cricket, a summer sport. Its rules are complicated and a game can take up to five days to complete. Other popular sports are tennis, golf, squash, darts, track, badminton, wrestling, boxing, ice skating, car racing, polo, horse racing and jumping, and snooker, a version of pool. One of the country's fastest-growing sports is US style football, and many areas have their own team.

Land

Part of the island of Great Britain, England is bordered on the north by Scotland and on the west by Wales and the Atlantic Ocean. The North Sea to the east and the English Channel to the south separate England from the rest of Europe. No part of England is more than 70 miles (113 km) from the coast.

Slightly smaller than the state of Wisconsin, England's total land area is 50,400 square miles (130,400 sq km), making it one of Europe's smallest countries. It is divided into the lowland area of the south, east, and center and the highland area of the north and west. The north is mountainous with the spectacular Lake District and Pennine Range. The highest peak is Scafell Pike, about 3,200 feet (980 m) high. The lowland is a plain dotted with gently rolling hills.

Climate

Thanks to warm ocean currents and warm winds, England enjoys a mild climate. Temperatures rarely fall below 25°F (-4°C) in the winter or exceed 70°F (21°C) in the summer. The south is usually drier and slightly warmer than the north. Annual rainfall varies between 20 to 40 inches (51-102 cm).

Agriculture

England's agriculture is highly efficient and meets about 75% of the country's food requirements. Almost 80% of the land is devoted to agriculture yet only 2% of the work force is employed in farming. Farmers grow wheat, barley, oats, potatoes, oilseeds, and sugar beets and raise cattle, sheep, pigs, and poultry.

England is a member of the European Economic Community (EEC) and so trades its agricultural products without high tariffs with other member countries. At a typical English dinner, you might eat cheese from Holland, butter from Denmark, lamb from New Zealand, and fruit from France, Italy, or Spain.

ENGLAND — Political and Physical

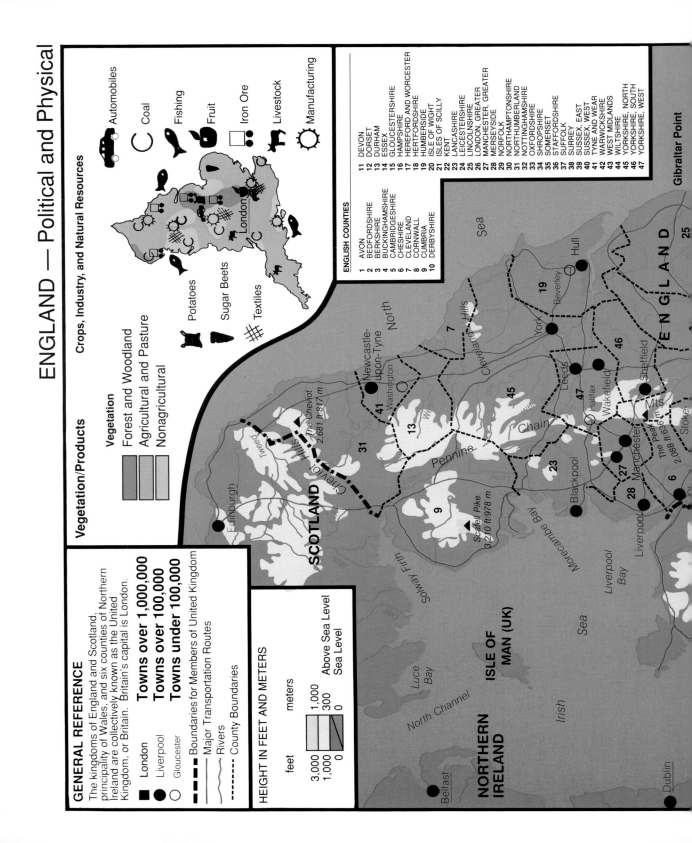

GENERAL REFERENCE

The kingdoms of England and Scotland, principality of Wales, and six counties of Northern Ireland are collectively known as the United Kingdom, or Britain. Britain's capital is London.

■ London   **Towns over 1,000,000**
● Liverpool   **Towns over 100,000**
○ Gloucester   **Towns under 100,000**

▪▪▪ Boundaries for Members of United Kingdom
— Major Transportation Routes
⁓ Rivers
- - - County Boundaries

HEIGHT IN FEET AND METERS

feet	meters	
3,000	1,000	Above Sea Level
1,000	300	
0	0	Sea Level

Vegetation/Products

Vegetation

Forest and Woodland
Agricultural and Pasture
Nonagricultural

Crops, Industry, and Natural Resources

Automobiles
Coal
Fishing
Fruit
Iron Ore
Livestock
Manufacturing

Potatoes
Sugar Beets
Textiles

London

ENGLISH COUNTIES

1	AVON
2	BEDFORDSHIRE
3	BERKSHIRE
4	BUCKINGHAMSHIRE
5	CAMBRIDGESHIRE
6	CHESHIRE
7	CLEVELAND
8	CORNWALL
9	CUMBRIA
10	DERBYSHIRE
11	DEVON
12	DORSET
13	DURHAM
14	ESSEX
15	GLOUCESTERSHIRE
16	HAMPSHIRE
17	HEREFORD AND WORCESTER
18	HERTFORDSHIRE
19	HUMBERSIDE
20	ISLE OF WIGHT
21	ISLES OF SCILLY
22	KENT
23	LANCASHIRE
24	LEICESTERSHIRE
25	LINCOLNSHIRE
26	LONDON, GREATER
27	MANCHESTER, GREATER
28	MERSEYSIDE
29	NORFOLK
30	NORTHAMPTONSHIRE
31	NORTHUMBERLAND
32	NOTTINGHAMSHIRE
33	OXFORDSHIRE
34	SHROPSHIRE
35	SOMERSET
36	STAFFORDSHIRE
37	SUFFOLK
38	SURREY
39	SUSSEX, EAST
40	SUSSEX, WEST
41	TYNE AND WEAR
42	WARWICKSHIRE
43	WEST MIDLANDS
44	WILTSHIRE
45	YORKSHIRE, NORTH
46	YORKSHIRE, SOUTH
47	YORKSHIRE, WEST

SCOTLAND

Edinburgh

Tweed

Cheviot Hills

The Cheviot 2,681 ft/817 m

Nith

Solway Firth

Eden

Scafel Pike 3,210 ft/978 m

Pennine

Chain

Lune

Morecambe Bay

Blackpool

Liverpool

Liverpool Bay

Irish Sea

ISLE OF MAN (UK)

NORTHERN IRELAND

Belfast

North Channel

Luce Bay

Dee

Dublin

Newcastle-upon-Tyne

Washington

North

Cleveland Hills

7

Wear

York

Leeds

Wakefield

Halifax

Manchester

The Peak 2,088 ft/636 m

Mts.

Stoke

Sheffield

Beverley

Hull

Sea

ENGLAND

Gibraltar Point

25

19

45

47

46

41

31

13

9

23

27

28

6

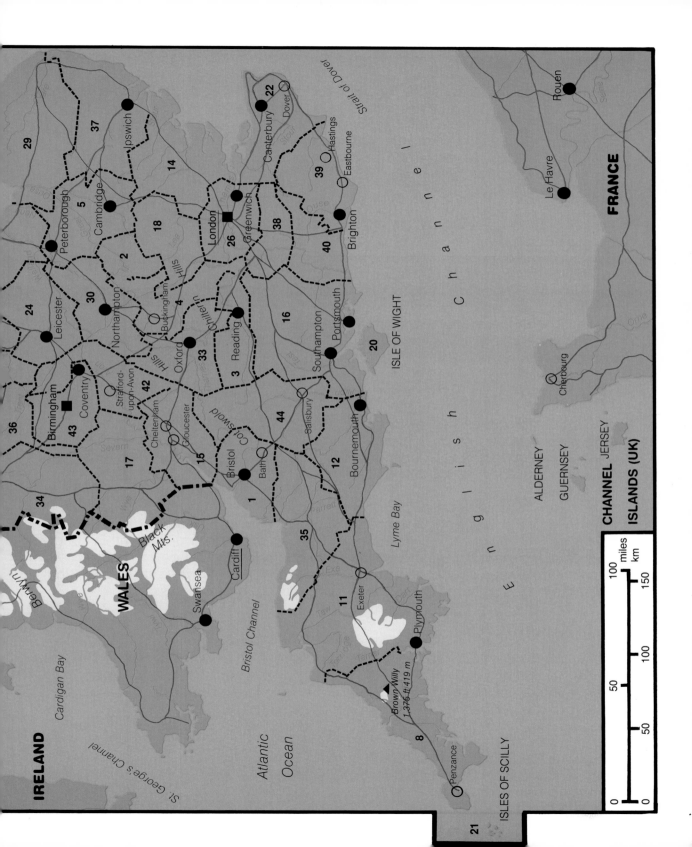

IRELAND

Cardigan Bay

St. George's Channel

Berwyn

WALES

Black
Mts.

34

36

Swansea

Cardiff

Bristol Channel

Atlantic
Ocean

35

Lyme Bay

ISLES OF SCILLY

21

Penzance

8

Brown Willy
1,376 ft 419 m

Plymouth

11

Exeter

Severn

Wye

17

1

15

Bath

Bristol

Gloucester

Cheltenham

42

Stratford-
upon-Avon

Birmingham

43

Coventry

Cotswold

44

12

Bournemouth

Salisbury

3

Reading

Oxford

33

Chiltern

Hills

Buckingham

4

Northampton

30

Leicester

24

Peterborough

5

Cambridge

29

37

Ipswich

14

18

2

London

26

Greenwich

38

40

Brighton

16

Southampton

Portsmouth

20

ISLE OF WIGHT

Eastbourne

Hastings

39

Canterbury

Dover

22

Strait of Dover

English Channel

CHANNEL
ISLANDS (UK)

JERSEY

GUERNSEY

ALDERNEY

Cherbourg

FRANCE

Le Havre

Rouen

Seine

Orne

0   50   100 miles
0   50   100   150 km

Natural Resources and Industry

England's natural resources have long been a source of wealth for the country. Since before Roman times, miners have quarried copper, lead, and iron. For centuries, tin mining in Cornwall provided most of the world's tin. England also produces zinc, lead, limestone, and sand and has small deposits of gold, silver, copper, and potash. Since the 1970s, North Sea oil and gas fields have helped make England self-sufficient in energy. In 1988, about 18% of its electricity came from nuclear power.

This variety of natural resources provides a basis for a number of privately and publicly owned industries. With its ports of London, Liverpool, and Southampton, England can easily trade its manufactured goods with other nations. It exports vehicles, iron, steel, machinery, chemicals, locomotives, ships, drugs, televisions, radios, weapons, scientific instruments, jet aircraft, farming machinery, woolen and synthetic textiles, and radar and navigation equipment. Its main trading partners are the US, West Germany, France, and the Netherlands. England also has a strong tourism industry. And the seemingly endless supply of North Sea fish has made fishing a staple industry.

Population and Ethnic Groups

Just over 46 million people live in England — about 80% of them in cities and towns. The population growth rate is now close to zero and is the second lowest in the world. The population density is 918 people per square mile (355 people per sq km), compared to just 66 per square mile (25.5 per sq km) in the US.

Most people are Caucasian, although since World War II, many British subjects from Commonwealth countries and former territories in Africa, the West Indies, and Asia have come to find work. They tend to make their own communities within London and in urban areas in the north and the Midlands in England's center. Some feel they are unfairly treated in such issues as housing, welfare, and employment. In the 1980s, this led to some racial tension and rioting in the streets of London.

Art and Culture

Over thousands of years, successive waves of European peoples introduced their art and customs to England. The Romans built amphitheaters, villas, and heated baths. Many examples of their culture can be seen in London, York, Chester, and Bath. From the 7th century on, masons constructed religious buildings like abbeys, cathedrals, and churches all over England. During the Middle Ages, sturdy castles, majestic cathedrals such as those in Canterbury and Durham, and magnificent abbeys like Westminster Abbey and Fountains in Yorkshire, rose against the sky. Perhaps England's greatest architect was Sir Christopher Wren, whose masterpiece is St. Paul's Cathedral in London.

Students all over North America often read works by three of England's greatest poets and novelists. Geoffrey Chaucer (1340-1400) wrote *The Canterbury Tales*, giving a vivid picture of English life in the 14th century. William Shakespeare (1564-1616), England's most widely read poet and dramatist, penned classic plays like *Romeo and Juliet*, *Hamlet*, and *Macbeth*. Victorian novelist Charles Dickens (1812-1870) wrote great fat novels filled with interesting characters. His novel *Oliver Twist* was made into the popular musical *Oliver!* and *A Christmas Carol*, with Tiny Tim, Bob Cratchit, and Scrooge, has become a Christmas classic.

London is the cultural center of the realm, famous for its theaters, galleries, and museums. Some famous art buildings are the National Theatre, the Royal Opera House, and the Royal Albert Hall. English plays and movies are respected worldwide, and actors such as Sir Laurence Olivier and Sir John Gielgud are internationally famous for their stage and movie performances. British studios provide filming facilities for many US films, including the *Star Wars* trilogy.

England has also produced world-class musicians. In classical music, the operas of Benjamin Britten and orchestral compositions by Sir William Walton are especially popular. And there can be few people who haven't heard of the Beatles or the Rolling Stones! England has also exported musicals by Andrew Lloyd Webber, including *Jesus Christ Superstar*, *Cats*, and *The Phantom of the Opera*.

London

English author Samuel Johnson said, "When a man is tired of London he is tired of life; for there is in London all that life can afford." While Dr. Johnson might not recognize his London now, with its skyline of tower blocks rather than spires and church towers, London still offers people the same variety of life.

London is not one city, but rather a series of cities, villages, and neighborhoods, many with their own distinct industries, atmospheres, and ethnic populations. They stretch out from the central point of the City of London itself. One square mile (2.6 sq km) in size, this area is the site of an original Roman town.

Hamleys of Regent Street, Ltd. This London landmark is famous for its equipment for all kinds of sports and its fabulous variety of toys.

Nearby is the City of Westminster with the Houses of Parliament. Big Ben, the main bell of the clock tower, presides over meetings. Another tower, the Tower of London, has served as a home for royalty and also as their prison and execution site.

Teeming with ships, the Thames River winds through the city, among stately buildings, modern skyscrapers, and massive monuments attesting to the extent of the British Empire. You can walk along the Thames at night and survey buildings like the Royal Festival Hall, structures like the Albert Bridge, and monuments like the statue of Bodicea, an early warrior queen, sparkling with light. Walk west from the river and see Buckingham Palace and Hyde Park, with its Speakers' Corner where anyone can make a speech on any topic — as long as they can stand the hecklers.

The quiet of the night gives little hint of the bustling streets during the day. Black taxicabs crowd the streets, especially during rush hour, while motorcycle taxis twist through the gridlocked traffic. Tourists also throng much of London, visiting galleries, monuments, and museums such as the British Museum, housing one of the world's finest libraries plus an outstanding collection of artwork, antiquities, and objects of natural history. Art exhibits abound, from the classical collections at the National Gallery to the romantic, impressionistic, and modern art collections of the Tate to the experimental art of the galleries of Whitechapel.

The English in North America

The English were among the first Europeans to settle in North America. John Cabot, an Englishman, reached the mainland in 1497, so England claimed the continent as its own. The first wave of English immigrants were the Pilgrims, Puritans who fled the religious persecution of Charles I. Other English people soon followed, seeking land to farm and freedom from governmental control and from religious turmoil.

England wanted Canada for its farmland, its lucrative fur trade, and its abundant fishing, but France had the same goals. The English fought the French in North America during the late 17th and early 18th centuries and forced France to relinquish territories on the entire continent.

Over the next century and a half, more English came to seek their fortune in North America. By the late 20th century, people of British origins formed 40% of the Canadian population and almost 20% of all US citizens.

Besides giving the US its official language and Canada one of its two languages, the English influenced North American architecture, art, fashion, literature, music, movies, and television. English television series such as "Upstairs, Downstairs," "Monty Python's Flying Circus," "Fawlty Towers," and "EastEnders" entertain viewers across North America and set standards of excellence for television production.

Glossary of Useful English Terms

Oscar Wilde, the nineteenth-century humorist, once said that "the English have really everything in common with the Americans, except of course language." Looking at some of the words below, it is easy to see what he meant.

bobby	policeman
bonnet	car hood
boot	car trunk
cheers	thank you; goodbye
chemist	druggist
chips	French fries
cooker	stove
crisps	potato chips
draughts	checkers
fortnight	two weeks
jumper	sweater
lift	elevator
loo	toilet
lorry	truck
motorway	freeway
petrol	gasoline
sledge	sled
spanner	wrench
sweets	candy
Ta	thanks
turn-ups	pant cuffs
vest	undershirt
windscreen	windshield

More Books About England

Here are more books about England and the United Kingdom. If you are interested in them, check your local library or bookstore. Some of these books may be helpful in doing research for the "Things to Do" projects that follow.

The Crack in the Teacup: Britain in the Twentieth Century. Warner (Houghton Mifflin)
The Door in the Wall. De Angeli (Scholastic)
Drums and Trumpets: The House of Stuart. McLeod (Houghton Mifflin)
England. Greene (Childrens Press)
Growing up in Puritan Times. Clarke (David & Charles)
Life in Roman Britain. Birley (David & Charles)
A Mighty Ferment: Britain in the Age of Revolution. Snodin (Houghton Mifflin)
Passport to Great Britain. Langley (Franklin Watts)
The Story of an English Village. Goodall (Macmillan)

Things to Do — Research Projects

England's empire building changed people's lives in countries around the world. Now people from those colonized countries are entering England, rapidly changing its character and culture. As you read about events that have shaped modern England, remember the importance of accurate, up-to-date information from other sources. Two such publications your library may have will tell you about recent newspaper and magazine articles on many topics:

Readers' Guide to Periodical Literature
Children's Magazine Guide

1. The slave trade for England, though shameful, was profitable. Why did slavery stop in England and North America and when?

2. The Industrial Revolution in England was a time of great progress and poverty. What was life like for children in those times?

3. Learn more about the English film industry. Why do so many US filmmakers have their movies edited and their special effects created in England?

More Things to Do — Activities

These projects are designed to make you think more about England. They offer interesting ideas for group or individual work at school or at home.

1. Would you like to be a prince or princess, a king or a queen? What do you think life must be like for Prince Charles and Princess Diana?

2. Once, the British Empire spread across much of the world. Choose a former English colony other than your own and compare life before and after the English arrived there.

3. In medieval England, the abbeys were important centers of art and agriculture. Who lived in abbeys? What were their lives like?

4. For a pen pal in England, write to these people:

International Pen Friends
P.O. Box 290065
Brooklyn, New York 11229-0001

Worldwide Pen Friends
P.O. Box 39097
Downey, CA 90241

Be sure to tell them from what country you want your pen pal. Also include your full name and address.

Index

63